E S T A T E   P U B ... T I O N S

HUNTINGDON · S

ST IVES   GODMANCHESTER

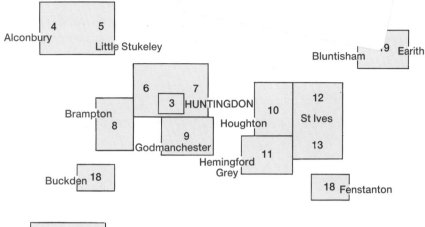

| 4 | 5 |
| Alconbury | Little Stukeley |

Bluntisham   .9 Earith

| 6 | 7 |
| 3 | HUNTINGDON |
Brampton
| 8 |
Houghton
| 10 |
| 12 |
St Ives

| 9 |
Godmanchester
| 11 |
| 13 |
Hemingford Grey

Buckden 18

18 Fenstanton

| 14 | 15 |
Eaton Ford
| 3 |
Eaton Socon 16 | 17 |
ST NEOTS

Every effort has been made to verify the accuracy of information in this book but the publishers cannot accept responsibility for expense or loss caused by any error or omission. Information that will be of assistance to the user of the maps will be welcomed.

The representation of a road, track or footpath on the maps in this atlas is no evidence of the existence of a right of way.

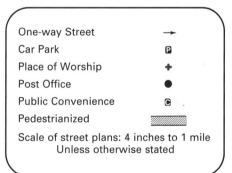

One-way Street	→
Car Park	℗
Place of Worship	✚
Post Office	●
Public Convenience	Ⓒ
Pedestrianized	▨

Scale of street plans: 4 inches to 1 mile
Unless otherwise stated

Street plans prepared and published by ESTATE PUBLICATIONS, Bridewell House, TENTERDEN, KENT, and based upon the ORDNANCE SURVEY mapping with the permission of The Controller of H. M. Stationery Office.

The publishers acknowledge the co-operation of the local authorities of towns represented in this atlas.

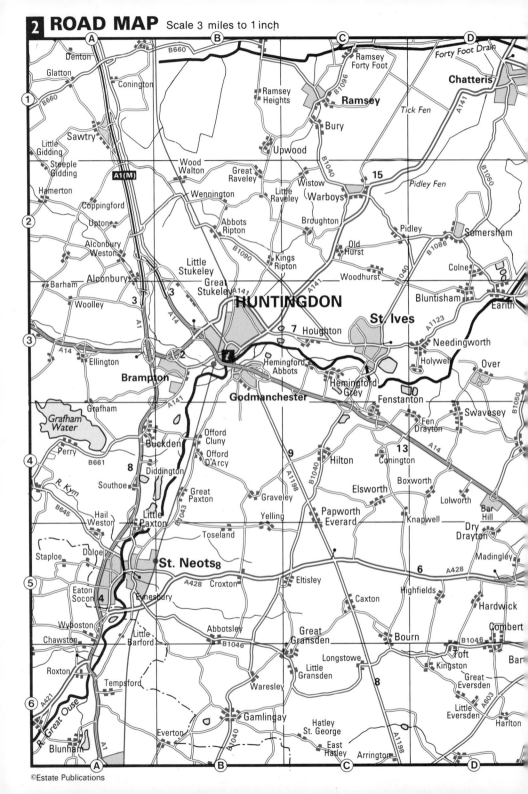

ale: 8 inches to 1 mile

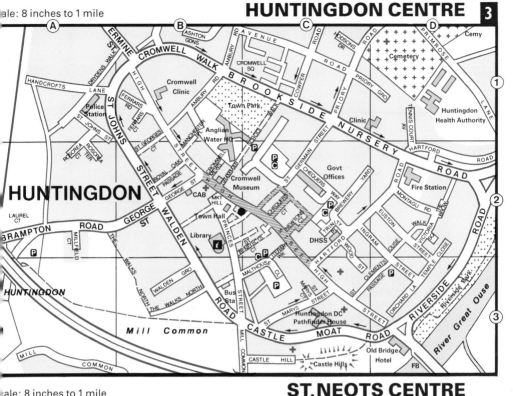

HUNTINGDON

ale: 8 inches to 1 mile

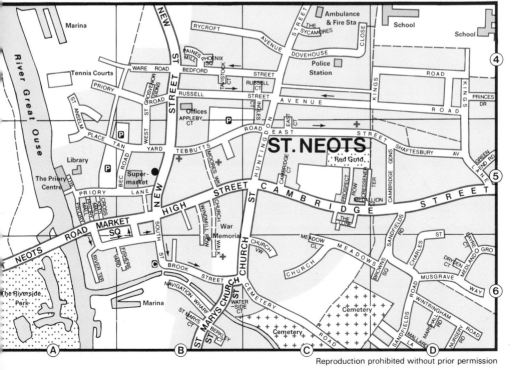

ST.NEOTS

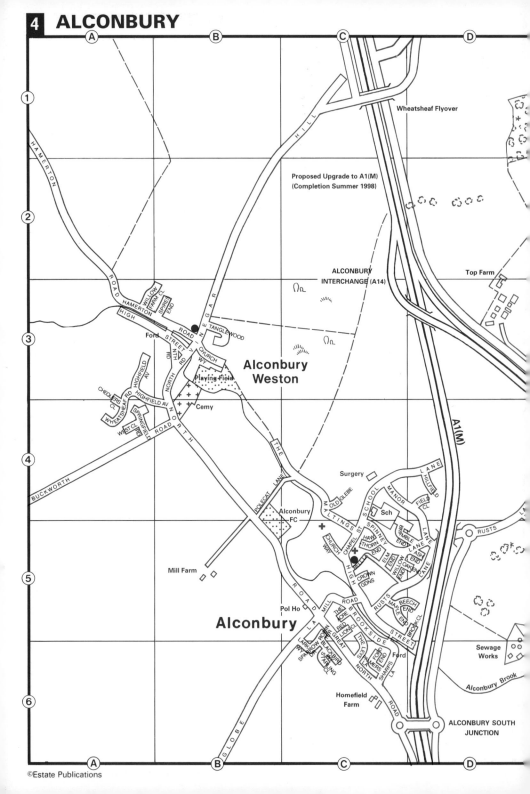

ermitage Wood

Long Coppice

ALCONBURY   AIRFIELD

RUSTS LANE
JUNCTION

Services

Home Farm

lconbury
House

Pringle
Farm

Little
Stukeley

Hall

Nook Farm

ERMINE

STREET

MILL RD

MILL CL

LOW ROAD

CHURCH ROAD

SHARPERS RD

PRINGLE WAY

PRINGLE CT

PRINGLE WAY

ALPHA LA

BRAVO LA

CEDAR DRIVE

ELM DRIVE

BIRCH DRIVE

DELTA

MAPLE DRIVE

ECHO LA

STREET

Warehouse

ERMINE BUSINESS CENTRE

ERMINE BUSINESS PARK

WASHINGLEY RD

LATHAM RD

THE INTERCHANGE IND EST

St JOHNS BUSINESS CENTRE

ANDERSON BUSINESS CENTRE

RETAIL PARK

Tower Square

ABBOTS RIPTON ROAD

KING

SPITTALS WAY

STUKELEY

SPITTALS

STREET

A14

STUKELEY MEADOWS IND EST

HALCYON COURT

Factories

Factories

HINCHINGBROOKE BUSINESS PARK

KINGFISHER WY

School

Recreation Centre

Stukeley

HUNTINGDON BUSINESS CENTRE

Playing Field

Views Common

School

CHERRY TREE CL

Spring or Horse Common

Laboratory

ERMINE STREET ROAD

HINCHINGBROOKE HOSPITAL

CROMWELL WK

Town Park

Cromwell Mus

Pol Sta

HINCHINGBROOKE

Constabulary HQ

Fire HQ

ST JOHNS ST

HIGH ST

WALDEN RD

BRAMPTON ROAD

Visitors Centre

Hinchingbrooke Country Park

School

PARK

Lodge CL

HEADLANDS AV

SCHOLARS

HUNTINGDON

Bus Sta

A14

Hinchingbrooke House & remains of Priory

MILL

COMMON

CASTL

©Estate Publications

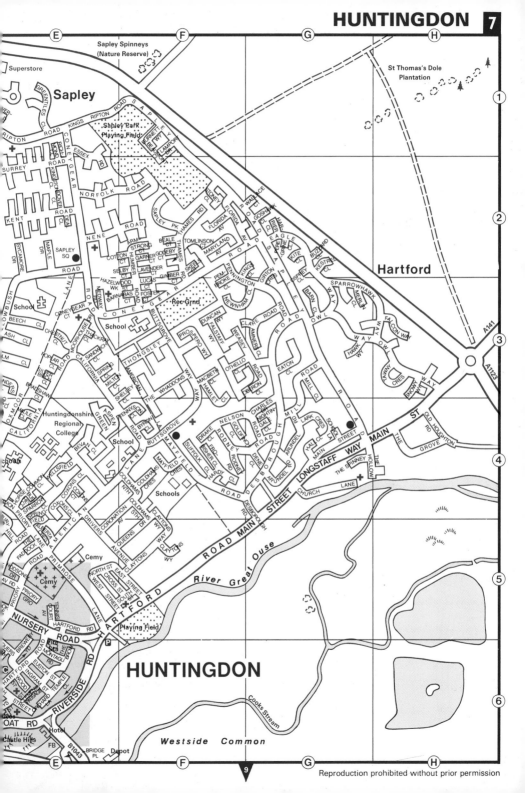

Sapley Spinneys
(Nature Reserve)

Superstore

St Thomas's Dole
Plantation

Sapley

Sapley Park
Playing Field

Hartford

Rec Grnd

School

School

Huntingdonshire
Regional
College

School

Schools

Cemy

Cemy

NURSERY ROAD

Playing Field

HUNTINGDON

River Great Ouse

Hotel

Castle Hills

FB

Depot

BRIDGE
PL

Westside Common

Cooks Stream

9

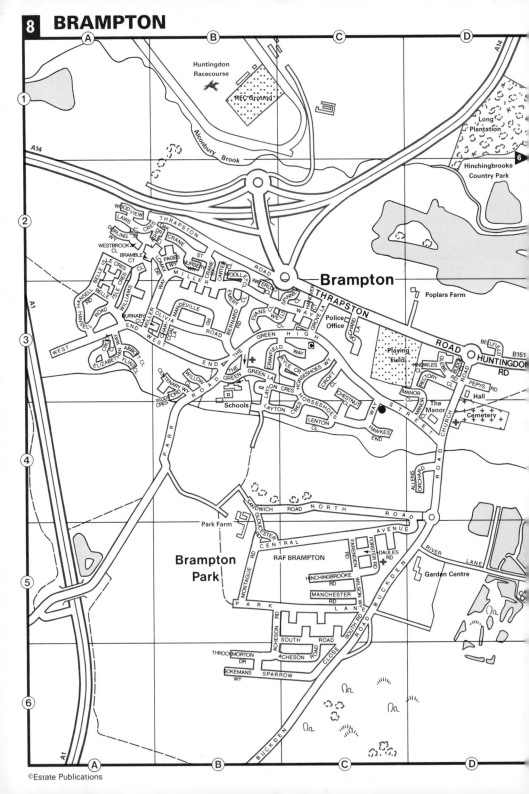

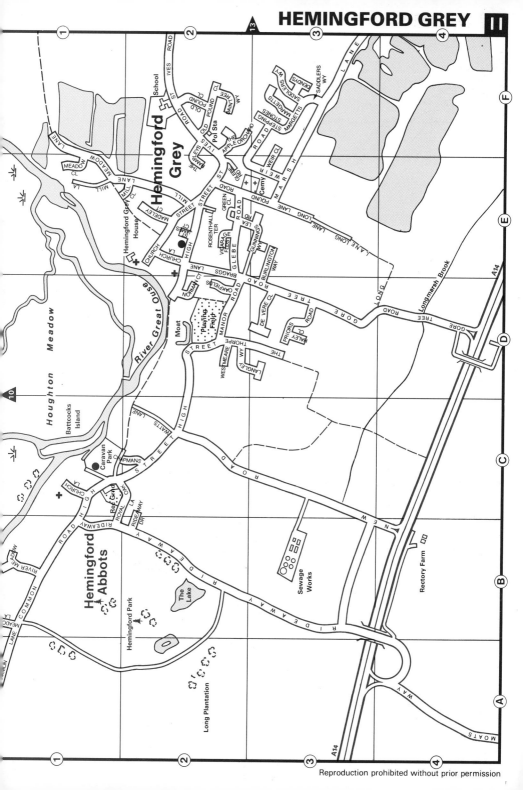

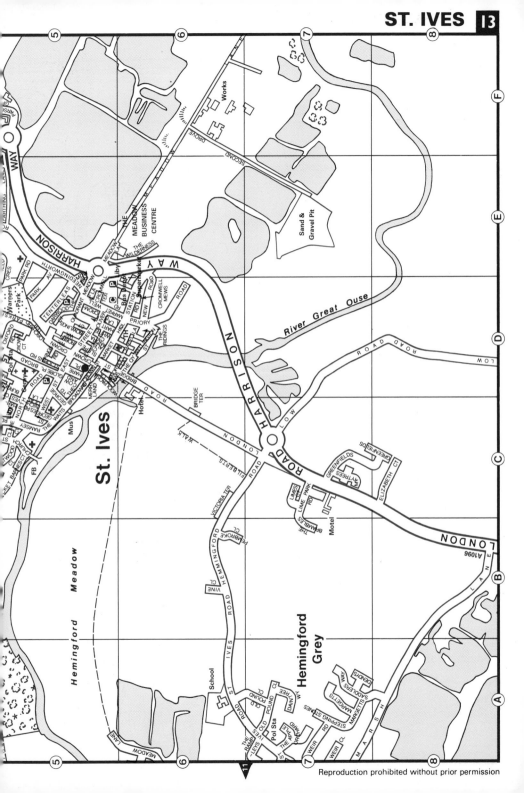

St. Ives

Hemingford Grey

Hemingford Meadow

River Great Ouse

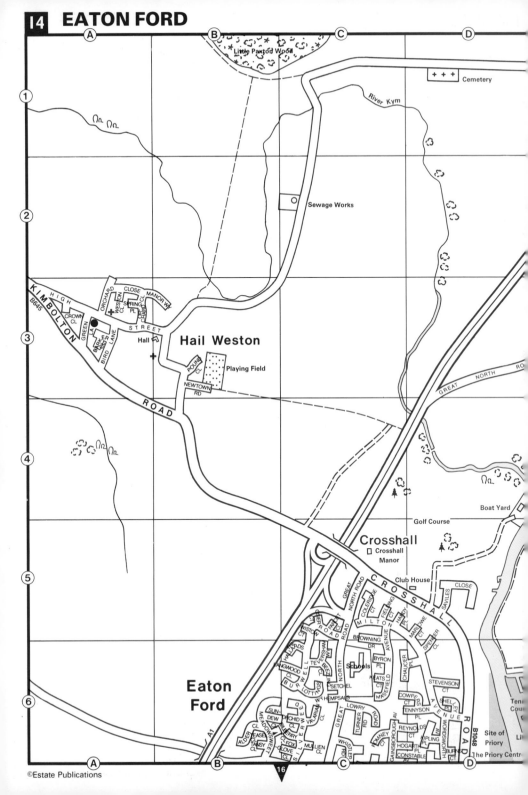

A B C D

Little Paxton Wood

Cemetery

River Kym

1

Sewage Works

2

KIMBOLTON B645

HIGH

ORCHARD
CLOSE
WESTON CL
SPRING PL
MANOR WY
CROWN CL
GREEN LA
BARKER CL
BIRD LANE
STREET

Hall

Hail Weston

3

POUND CT
NEWTOWN RD

Playing Field

ROAD

GREAT NORTH RD

4

Boat Yard

Golf Course

Crosshall
Crosshall Manor

Club House

CLOSE
SAVILES

5

Eaton Ford

A1

GREAT NORTH ROAD
CROSSHALL ROAD
MILTON AVENUE

COLERIDGE
FIELDING
HARDY
MARLOWE
SPENCER
CLEMER
BROWNING DR
BYRON PL
CHAUCER PL
WAKEFIELD
STEVENSON CT
SHEL
COWPER CT
ENNYSON CT
REYNOLDS CT
KIPLING PL
HOGARTH PL
CONSTABLE AV
BURNS

WISTOW
RICHARDS
LANGWOOD CL
BURWELL
LOTTINGS
HEMPSALS
SETCHEL
KEATS
WHI
GREAT NORTH ROAD
FRIEST ROAD
TEVERSHAM
WELL
GAINSBOROUGH AV
ROMNEY
TURNER RD
LOWRY RD
WORDSWORTH

SILVER
VARIAN
MULLIEN
SUN
DEW
ORCHID
BILBERRY CL
CLOVER
TEASEL
TANSY
MEADOWSWEET

Schools

Site of Priory
The Priory Centre
B1048

6

A B C D

16

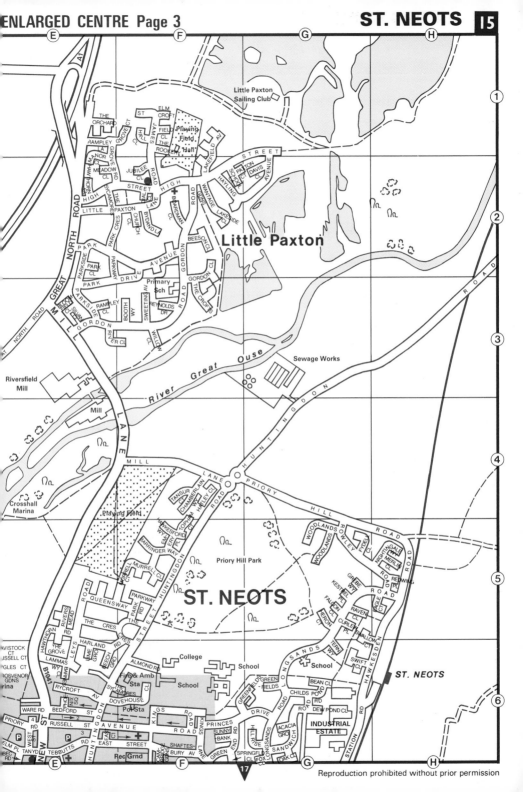

ST. NEOTS

Little Paxton

ST. NEOTS

Little Paxton Sailing Club

River Great Ouse

Sewage Works

Riversfield Mill

Mill

Crosshall Marina

Priory Hill Park

College

School

School

School

Fire & Amb Sta

Pol Sta

INDUSTRIAL ESTATE

ST. NEOTS

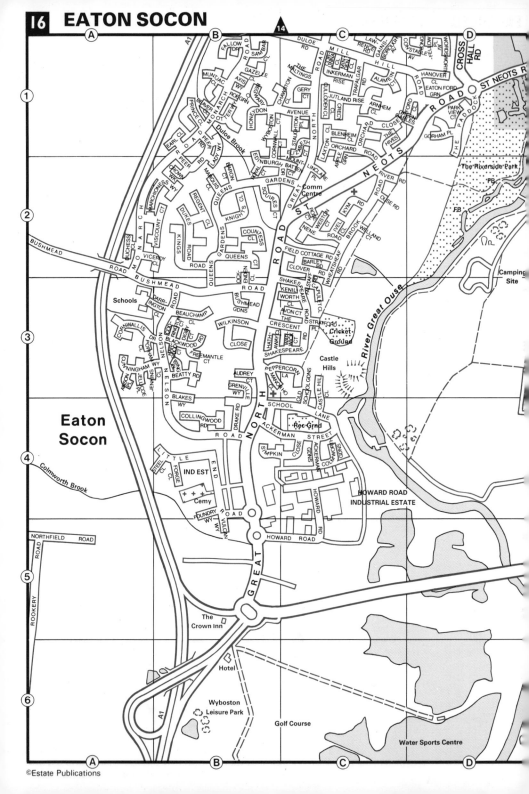

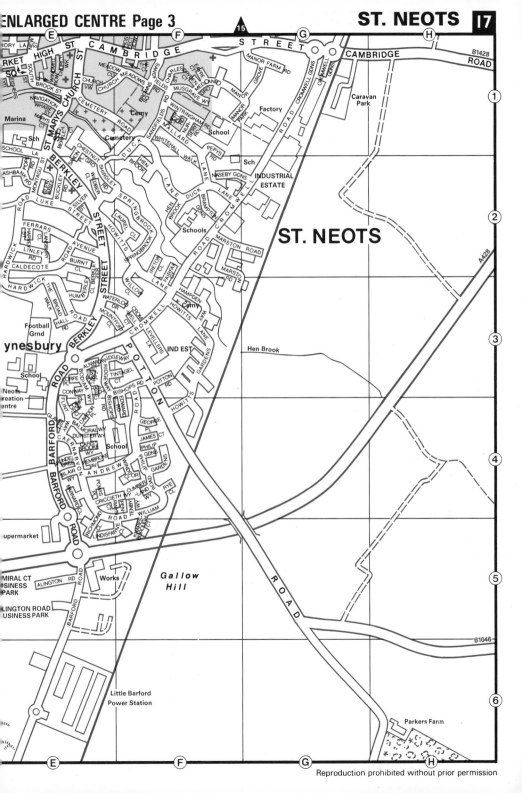

ST. NEOTS

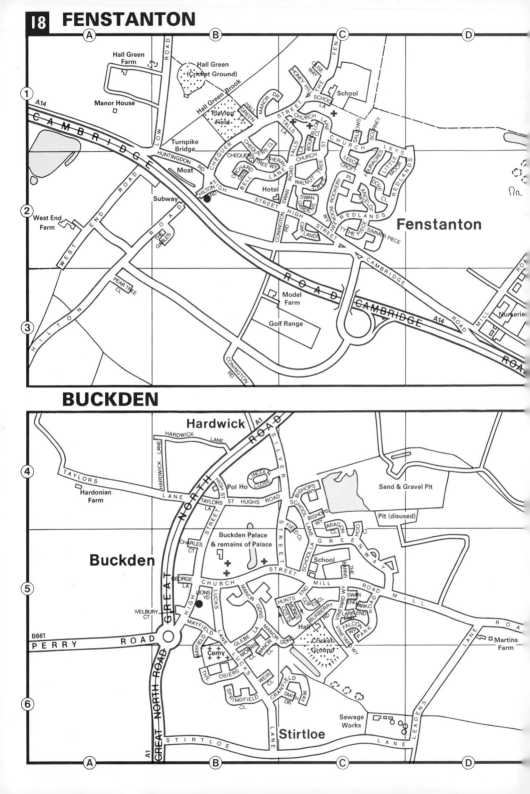

The Index includes some names for which there is insufficient space on the maps. These names are preceded by an * and are followed by the nearest adjoining thoroughfare.

HUNTINGDON

Abbots Ripton Rd. PE17   6 D1
Abbots Cres. PE17   12 C3
Abbott Clo. PE18   8 A3
Acacia Av. PE17   12 B3
Adelaide Wk. PE17   19 F3
Alabama Way. PE17   12 A3
Albemarle Rd. PE17   12 C2
Alberta Cres. PE18   7 E5
Alexandra Ct. PE17   13 D5
All Saints Clo. PE17   12 D3
All Saints Grn. PE17   12 D3
Allen Farm Clo. PE18   9 C3
Allens Orchard. PE18   8 D4
Almond Clo. PE18   9 D2
Alms Clo. PE18   6 C3
Alpha La. PE17   5 H6
Alwyn Clo. PE17   12 D2
Ambury Hill. PE18   6 D5
Ambury Rd. PE18   3 B1
American La. PE18   7 E5
Amners Clo. PE18   7 G3
Anderson Cres. PE18   9 D2
Ansley Rd. PE17   10 C5
Ansley Way. PE17   12 A3
Anson Dri. PE17   12 C2
Aragon Clo. PE18   18 C5
Archers Ct. PE18   6 C4
Armstrong Ct. PE18   7 F2
Arran Way. PE17   12 C1
Arundel Rd. PE18   7 G4
Ash Clo. PE18   7 E3
Ash Ct. PE18   8 B2
Ash End. PE17   4 D5
Aspen Grn. PE17   7 E4
Astilbe La. PE18   6 D4
Audley Clo. PE17   12 A3
Avenue Rd. PE18   3 C1
Avro Ct. PE18   6 B2

Barn Clo. PE18   7 G3
Barnes Ct. PE17   13 C5
*Barringer Ct,
  London St. PE18   9 C3
Bascraft Way. PE18   9 D3
Bassenthwaite. PE18   6 B4
Bath Cres. PE17   10 C2
Bayliss. PE18   9 D4
Beacon Clo. PE18   6 B4
Beale Ct. PE18   7 F2
Beaumont Clo. PE18   7 F1
Bedford Av. PE17   10 C2
Bedford Cres. PE17   12 C1
Beech Clo. PE18   7 E3
Beech Dri. PE17   12 C3
Beech End. PE17   4 C5
Bell La, Alconbury. PE17   4 C5
Bell La, Fenstanton. PE18   18 B2
Belle Isle Cres. PE18   8 A2
Bellfield. PE18   8 D3
Bennett Rd. PE17   10 B1
Bergamont Clo. PE18   9 D4
Bernard Clo. PE18   7 E4
Bernard Rd. PE18   8 B3
Betts Clo. PE18   9 C3
Bevan Clo. PE17   7 E4
Birch Dri. PE17   5 H6
Bishops Way. PE18   18 C4
Bittern Clo. PE17   12 B2
Black Hill. PE17   12 B2
Blackbird Way. PE17   4 C6
Blackstone Rd. PE18   6 C3
Bleawater. PE18.   6 C4
Blenheim Dri. PE18   12 C2
Blenheim Way. PE17   10 B1
Blethan Dri. PE18   6 A3
Bluntisham Rd. PE17   19 B2

Boretree Way. PE17   6 A3
Bourdillon Clo. PE18   18 C1
Bowlings Ct. PE17   13 D5
Bradshaw Clo. PE18   7 E3
Braggs La. PE18   11 E2
Bramble Ct. PE18   8 A2
Bramble End. PE17   4 C5
Bramley Gro. PE17   19 B3
Bramley Rd. PE17   12 E4
Brampton Rd. PE18   3 A2
Bravo La. PE18   5 H6
Brecon Way. PE18   6 B6
Brewery Yd. PE18   3 C2
Brick Kilns. PE18   9 D4
Bridge End. PE17   19 E3
*Bridge Foot,
  The Quay. PE17   13 D6
*Bridge House,
  The Quay. PE17   13 D6
Bridge St. PE17   13 D6
Bridge Ter. PE17   13 C6
Brigland Clo. PE18   6 B3
Broad Leas. PE17   12 D4
*Broad Leas Ct,
  Broad Leas. PE17   12 D4
Brook Clo. PE17   4 D5
Brookside, Alconbury. PE17   4 C5
Brookside, Houghton. PE17   10 C5
Brookside, Huntingdon. PE18   3 B1
Broom Way. PE17   12 D3
Buckden Rd. PE18   8 B6
Buckworth Rd. PE17   4 A4
Budge Clo. PE18   8 D3
Bull La. PE17   13 D6
Burberry Rd. PE18   18 C5
Bure Clo. PE17   12 D2
Burgess Wk. PE17   13 D5
Burleigh Rd. PE17   12 C1
Burlington Way. PE18   11 E3
Burmoor Clo. PE18   6 B4
Burnaby Clo. PE18   8 A3
Burnett Way. PE18   7 F1
Burns Way. PE17   12 B3
Burrel Rd. PE17   12 E2
Bursellars. PE17   12 D3
Bury Clo. PE17   12 B3
Bury Way. PE17   12 B3
Bushey Clo. PE18   7 E4
Buttermel Clo. PE18   9 D4
Buttermere. PE18   6 B3
Buttsgrove Way. PE18   7 F3
Buzzard Clo, PE18   7 G2
Byron Clo. PE18   7 F4

California Rd,
  Huntingdon. PE18   7 E3
California Rd, St Ives. PE17   12 B3
Cam Rd. PE17   12 D2
Cambridge Rd,
  Fenstanton. PE18   18 A1
Cambridge Rd,
  Godmanchester. PE18   9 D2
Cambridge Sq. PE17   10 C2
Cambridge St. PE18   9 C2
Cambridge Villas. PE18   9 D2
Canberra Dri. PE17   12 C2
Canberra Way. PE17   10 B1
Cardinal Way. PE18   9 E3
Carnaby Clo. PE17   9 D3
Carter St. PE18   8 B2
Castle Hill. PE18   3 C3
*Castle Hill Ct,
  High St. PE18   3 C3
Castle Moat Rd. PE18   3 C3
Cat La. PE17   19 A1
Causeway. PE18   7 E4
Caxton Rd. PE17   12 E3
Cedar Dri. PE17   5 H6
Cedar Rd. PE17   12 C3
Centenary Way. PE18   8 B3
Central Av. PE18   8 B5
Centurion Way. PE18   9 E3
Chadley La. PE18   9 C2
Chancellor Clo. PE18   6 C3
*Chapel Ct, Chapel La. PE17   13 D6
Chapel La, Houghton. PE17   10 B5
Chapel La, St Ives. PE17   13 D6

Chapel Rd. PE17   19 E3
Chapel St. PE17   4 C5
Chapmans. PE18   11 C2
Charcoal La. PE18   8 B3
Charles Ct. PE18   18 B5
Charles Dri. PE17   7 G4
Chaucer Way. PE17   12 B3
Chelmer Clo. PE17   12 E2
Chequer St. PE18   18 B2
Chequers Clo,
  Alconbury Weston. PE17   4 A3
Chequers Clo,
  Fenstanton. PE18   18 B1
Chequers Ct,
  Fenstanton. PE18   18 B2
Chequers Ct,
  Huntingdon. PE18   3 C2
Chequers Way. PE18   3 C2
Cherry Tree Clo. PE18   6 D4
Cherry Tree Way. PE18   18 B2
Chester Way. PE17   10 B2
Chester Way. PE18   9 E3
Chestnut Clo,
  Brampton. PE18   8 C4
Chestnut Clo,
  Huntingdon. PE18   7 E3
Chestnut Clo, St Ives. PE17   12 C3
Chestnut Rd. PE17   12 C3
Church La, Fenstanton. PE18   18 C1
Church La, Hartford. PE18   7 G4
Church La,
  Hemingford Abbots. PE18   11 C1
Church La,
  Hemingford Grey. PE18   11 E2
Church Leys. PE18   18 C1
Church Pl. PE18   9 C2
Church Rd. PE18   8 D4
Church St, Buckden. PE18   18 B5
Church St, Fenstanton. PE18   18 C2
Church St,
  Hemingford Grey. PE18   11 E2
Church St, St Ives. PE17   13 C5
Church Walk. PE17   10 A5
Church Way, Alconbury. PE17   4 C5
Church Way,
  Alconbury Weston. PE17   4 B3
Church Way,
  Little Stukeley. PE17   5 G6
Churchill Av. PE17   10 C2
*Churchill Hall, St Ives
  Business Pk. PE17   12 F4
Clare Ct. PE17   13 C5
*Clare Hall, St Ives
  Business Pk. PE17   12 F4
Clare Rd. PE17   7 G3
Claytons Way. PE18   7 F5
Clifton Rd. PE18   6 D3
Cob Pl. PE18   9 C4
Cohort Way. PE18   9 E2
Coldhams Cres. PE18   7 F4
Coldhams Nth. PE18   7 F4
Coldhams Sth. PE18   7 F4
Colne Rd, Bluntisham. PE17   19 B3
Colne Rd, Earith. PE17   19 D2
Colour Clo. PE18   6 D3
Comet Way. PE17   12 C2
Common La. PE18   11 A1
Coneygear Ct. PE18   7 E3
Coneygear Rd. PE18   7 E1
Conington Rd. PE18   18 B2
Coniston Clo. PE18   6 C3
Constable Rd. PE17   12 C2
Cooks Drove. PE17   19 F2
Copes Clo. PE18   18 C5
Copperbeech Clo. PE17   12 D4
Cordell Clo. PE17   12 B3
Cornwall Rd. PE17   10 B1
Corpus Christi La. PE18   9 C3
Cottage La. PE17   10 C4
Cotton Ct. PE18   7 F2
Cow and Hare Pl. PE17   13 D5
Cow La. PE18   9 E2
Cowper Rd. PE18   3 C1
Coxons Clo. PE17   7 E4
Coxons Ct. PE18   7 E4
Crane St. PE18   8 B2

Cranfield. PE18   18 C
Cranfield Way,
  Brampton. PE18   8 B
Cranfield Way,
  Buckden. PE18   18 B
Croft Clo. PE18   8 C
Croftfield Rd. PE18   9 D
Cromwell Mews,
  Huntingdon. PE18   3 B
Cromwell Mews,
  St Ives. PE17   13 D
Cromwell Pl. PE17   13 D
Cromwell Sq. PE18   3 C
Cromwell Ter. PE17   13 D
Cromwell Wk. PE18   3 B
Croot Clo. PE18   8 A
Cross St. PE18   7 E
Crowhill. PE18   9 C
*Crown Clo,
  Broad Leas. PE17   13 D
Crown Ct. PE17   13 D
Crown Gdns. PE17   4 C
Crown Pl. PE17   13 D
Crown St. PE17   13 D
Crown Wk. PE17   13 D
Crummock Water. PE18   6 C
Cumberland Clo. PE18   10 B
Curlew Clo. PE17   12 B

Da Vinci Clo. PE17   12 C
Daintree Way. PE18   11 F
*Dallington Ct,
  Trinity Pl. PE18   3 C
Darford. PE17   19 E
Dart Clo. PE17   12 E
Dartmoor Dri. PE18   6 B
Darwood Ct. PE17   13 D
Daules Rd. PE18   8 C
De Vere Clo. PE18   11 D
Deal Clo. PE18   7 E
Deben Av. PE17   12 D
Degas Dri. PE17   12 D
Deighton Clo. PE17   12 D
Delta Dri. PE17   5 H
Dendys. PE18   11 F
Dene Clo. PE18   7 G
Derwent Clo, St Ives. PE17   12 E
Derwent Clo, Stukeley. PE18   6 B
Desborough Rd. PE18   7 G
Devana Clo. PE18   9 C
Devoke Clo. PE18   6 C
Devon Clo. PE17   12 C
Devon Rd. PE17   10 B
Dorchester Way. PE17   10 B
Dorling Way. PE18   8 A
Dove Clo. PE18   18 C
Dovehouse Clo. PE18   9 D
Dover Clo. PE18   7 E
Dovey Clo. PE17   12 D
*Downing Hall, St Ives
  Business Pk. PE17   12 F
Drake Clo. PE18   7 F
Drivers Av. PE18   7 E
Druce Av. PE17   10 B
Drury La. PE17   19 B
Dryden Clo. PE17   12 B
Drydens Wk. PE18   3 A
Duck End. PE18   9 C
*Duncan Ho, High St,
  Earith. PE17   19 E
Duncan Way. PE18   7 F
Dunholt Way. PE17   19 C
Durham Way. PE17   10 C

Eagle Way. PE18   7 G
Earith Fen Drove. PE17   19 F
Earith Rd. PE17   19 C
Earning St. PE18   9 D
East Chadley La. PE17   9 D
East St, Bluntisham. PE17   19 A
East St, Colne. PE17   19 B
East St, Huntingdon. PE18   7 F
East St, St Ives. PE17   13 D
Eaton Clo. PE18   7 G
Echo La. PE17   5 H
Edinburgh Dri. PE17   12 C
Edison Rd. PE17   12 E

Edwards Wk. PE17	19 E3	
Elizabeth Ct. PE17	13 C7	
Elizabeth Way. PE17	19 C1	
Elizabethan Way. PE18	8 A3	
Elm Clo. PE18	7 E3	
Elm Dri. PE17	12 C3	
Elm Dri. PE17	5 H6	
Elm End. PE17	4 C5	
Elsworth Clo. PE17	12 E4	
Emery Clo. PE18	8 B3	
Emmanuel Hall, St Ives Business Pk. PE17	12 F4	
Ennerdale Clo. PE18	6 B4	
Erica Rd. PE17	12 D3	
Ermine Ct, Ermine St. PE18	6 D4	
Ermine St, Gt Stukeley. PE17	6 A1	
Ermine St, Huntingdon. PE18	3 B1	
Ermine St, Little Stukeley. PE17	5 G5	
Essex Rd. PE18	7 E1	
Euston St. PE18	3 D2	
Evans Clo. PE18	8 B3	
Exmoor Clo. PE18	6 B6	
Fairey Av. PE18	9 D3	
Fairfield. PE17	12 B3	
Fairfields. PE17	12 D4	
Fairfields Cres. PE17	13 E5	
Falcon Way, Buckden. PE18	18 C5	
Falcon Way, Hartford. PE18	7 H3	
Falstaff Way. PE18	7 F3	
Farenden Rd. PE18	8 C5	
Farm Clo. PE17	10 B5	
Farthing La. PE17	13 E5	
Ferndown Dri. PE18	9 D4	
Ferrars Ct. PE18	3 B1	
Ferrars Rd. PE18	3 B1	
Field Clo, Alconbury. PE17	4 D4	
Field Clo, Buckden. PE18	18 C4	
Field Wk. PE18	9 D3	
Filberts Wk. PE17	13 C6	
Fishers Way. PE18	9 C4	
Flint Clo. PE18	8 A3	
Florida Av. PE18	7 F2	
Ford End. PE17	4 C6	
Forster Rd. PE18	8 C5	
Forsythia Rd. PE17	12 D3	
Foster Ct. PE18	7 F3	
Foundry Wk, Market Hill. PE17	13 D5	
Four Acres. PE18	18 C2	
Fox Gro. PE18	9 D3	
Fraser Dri. PE18	12 D2	
Free Church Pass, Market Hill. PE17	13 D5	
Frobisher Clo. PE18	7 F4	
Frogs Hall. PE17	19 B4	
Gainsborough Dri. PE17	12 D2	
Garden Clo. PE17	12 D3	
Garner Ct. PE18	7 F2	
George La. PE18	18 B5	
George St. PE18	3 B2	
George Yd. PE17	13 C5	
Gimber Ct. PE18	7 G2	
Glebe La. PE18	18 B5	
Glebe Rd, Brampton. PE18	8 D3	
Glebe Rd, Hemingford Grey. PE18	11 E2	
Glebe Rd, Huntingdon. PE18	6 D3	
Globe La. PE18	4 B6	
Gloucester Rd, Brampton. PE18	8 B4	
Gloucester Rd, Wyton. PE17	10 B2	
Godeby Ct. PE18	7 F2	
Golden Rod. PE18	9 D4	
Goldfinch Clo. PE18	7 F4	
Gore Tree Rd. PE18	11 D3	
Gorse Way. PE17	12 D3	
Goshawk Clo. PE18	7 G2	
Gosslan Clo. PE18	12 D3	
Grafton Clo. PE17	12 C1	
Grainger Av. PE18	9 D3	
Grammar School Wk. PE18	3 B2	
Granary Clo. PE18	9 C2	
Granta Clo. PE17	12 D2	
Grange Rd. PE18	6 B4	
Great Farthing Clo. PE17	12 E4	
Great How. PE17	12 B2	
Great North Rd, Alconbury. PE17	4 C5	
Great North Rd, Buckden. PE18	18 B5	
Great Northern St. PE18	6 D5	
Grebe Clo. PE17	12 C2	
Green Clo. PE18	11 E2	
Green End. PE17	6 A1	
Green How. PE17	12 B2	
Green La, Brampton. PE18	8 B3	
Green La, Houghton. PE17	10 B5	
Green Leys. PE17	12 C4	
Greendale. PE18	6 B4	
Greenfields, Earith. PE17	19 E3	
Greenfields, St Ives. PE17	13 C7	
Greengarth. PE17	12 D4	
Greentiles Clo. PE17	7 E1	
Greenway. PE18	18 C5	
Grove Ct. PE18	9 D2	
*Grove Ct, Broad Leas. PE17	13 D5	
Grove La. PE18	9 D2	
Gunnings Way. PE18	11 E3	
Haley Clo. PE18	11 D3	
Hall Clo. PE18	7 G4	
Hall Green La. PE18	18 B1	
Hamerton Rd. PE17	4 A3	
Hamlet Clo. PE18	7 F3	
Hampshire. PE17	10 C2	
Handcrofts La. PE18	3 A1	
Hanover Ct. PE18	8 C3	
Hansell Rd. PE18	8 A3	
Harding Way. PE17	12 E3	
Hardwick La. PE18	18 B4	
Hardy Clo. PE18	7 F4	
Harrier Clo. PE18	7 G2	
Harris Way. PE18	10 B1	
Harrison Way. PE17	12 F4	
Hartford Rd. PE18	3 C3	
Harvest Ct. PE17	13 C5	
Haweswater. PE18	6 C4	
Hawk Dri. PE17	10 B1	
Hawk Way. PE18	7 G3	
Hawkes End. PE18	8 C4	
Hawthorn End. PE17	4 C5	
Hawthorn Way. PE17	12 D3	
Hayling Clo. PE18	9 C4	
Hazel Way. PE17	12 D4	
Hazelwood Wk. PE17	7 F3	
Headlands. PE18	6 C6	
Heddon Way. PE17	12 E2	
Hemmingford Rd. PE17	13 B6	
Hereward. PE17	19 F3	
Hermitage Rd. PE17	19 F2	
Heron Way. PE17	12 B2	
High Leys. PE17	12 B4	
High St, Alconbury. PE17	4 C5	
High St, Alconbury Weston. PE17	4 A3	
High St, Bluntisham. PE17	19 A3	
High St, Brampton. PE18	8 C3	
High St, Buckden. PE18	18 B5	
High St, Colne. PE17	19 B1	
High St, Earith. PE17	19 D3	
High St, Fenstanton. PE18	18 B2	
High St, Hemingford Abbots. PE18	11 C1	
High St, Hemingford Grey. PE18	11 E2	
High St, Huntingdon. PE18	3 B1	
Highfield Av. PE17	4 A3	
Hill Estate. PE17	10 C5	
Hill Rise. PE17	12 B2	
Hillfield. PE17	4 D4	
Hilsdens Dri. PE18	9 D2	
Hilton Rd. PE18	18 A3	
Hinchingbrooke Pk Rd. PE18	6 B5	
Hinchingbrooke Rd. PE18	8 C5	
Hodsons Dri. PE18	3 C1	
Hogarth Clo. PE17	12 D2	
Holbein Clo. PE17	12 D2	
Hollidays Rd. PE17	19 B3	
Holme Fen Drove. PE17	19 C1	
Holmehill. PE18	9 C4	
Home Farm Rd. PE17	10 B4	
Honey Hill. PE18	18 C1	
Hoo Clo. PE18	18 C5	
Horse Common Clo. PE18	7 E4	
Horse Common La. PE18	6 D4	
Horseshoes Way. PE18	8 C3	
Houghton Hill Rd. PE17	10 C5	
Houghton Rd. PE17	12 A4	
Hudpool. PE18	9 D4	
Humber Rd. PE18	7 F2	
Huntingdon Rd, Brampton. PE18	8 D3	
Huntingdon Rd, Fenstanton. PE18	18 B2	
Huntingdon Rd, Houghton. PE17	10 A4	
Hunts End. PE18	18 C5	
Hurricane Clo. PE18	6 C2	
Hurstingstone. PE17	12 C3	
Ilex Rd. PE17	12 D3	

INDUSTRIAL ESTATES:

Anderson Business Centre. PE18	6 C3	
Cardinal Distrib. Pk. PE18	9 F3	
Chord Business Pk. PE18	9 D4	
Earith Business Pk. PE17	19 F2	
Ermine Business Centre. PE18	6 C2	
Ermine Business Pk. PE18	6 C2	
Halcyon Ct. PE18	6 C3	
Hinchingbrooke Business Pk. PE17	6 A4	
Huntingdon Business Centre. PE18	6 C4	
St Ives Business Pk. PE17	12 F4	
St Johns Business Centre. PE17	6 C2	
Stukeley Meadows Ind Est. PE17	6 C3	
The Interchange Ind Est. PE17	6 C2	
The Meadow Business Centre. PE17	13 E6	
Ingram St. PE18	3 C2	
Ivelbury Ct. PE18	18 B5	
Kendall Way. PE17	10 B1	
Kent Clo. PE17	12 C1	
Kent Rd. PE18	7 E2	
Kestrel Clo, Hartford. PE18	7 G2	
Kestrel Clo, St Ives. PE17	12 B2	
Kiln Clo. PE18	12 B3	
*King George Ct, George La. PE18	18 B5	
Kingfisher Gro. PE17	12 C2	
Kingfisher Way. PE18	6 A4	
Kings Clo. PE18	7 F2	
Kings Gdns. PE18	6 D5	
*Kings Hall, St Ives Business Pk. PE17	12 F4	
Kings Hedges. PE17	12 C3	
Kings Rd. PE17	13 D5	
Kings Ripton Rd. PE17	6 D1	
Kingsbrook. PE17	12 D3	
Kisby Av. PE18	9 E2	
Kite Clo. PE18	7 G2	
Knowles Clo. PE18	8 D3	
Kyle Cres. PE18	8 C3	
Lake Way. PE18	6 C4	
Lakeview Ct. PE18	6 C2	
Lammas Gdns. PE18	6 D5	
Lammas Way. PE18	12 C4	
Lamport Dri. PE18	7 F1	
Lancaster Dri. PE17	12 C2	
Lancaster Rd. PE17	10 B1	
Lancaster Way, Godmanchester. PE18	9 D2	
Lancaster Way, Huntingdon. PE18	6 B2	
Lancelot Way. PE18	18 C2	
Landcliffe Clo. PE17	12 D3	
Langley Clo. PE18	12 C4	
Langley Ct. PE17	12 C4	
Langley Way. PE18	11 D2	
Lark Cres. PE18	7 G4	
Lark End. PE18	18 C5	
Lark Way. PE17	4 C6	
Laroc Ct. PE18	9 C3	
Latham Rd. PE18	6 C2	
Laughtons La. PE17	10 B5	
Laurel Ct. PE18	3 A2	
Lavender Ct. PE18	7 F2	
Lavender Way. PE17	12 D3	
Laws Cres. PE18	8 A2	
Layton Clo. PE18	8 B3	
Lea Rd. PE18	11 E2	
Leadens La. PE18	18 D6	
Leechcroft. PE18	3 C1	
Leger Clo. PE17	12 C3	
Legion Way. PE18	9 E3	
Lenton Pl. PE18	8 C4	
Levers Water. PE18	6 C5	
Lilac Way. PE17	12 D3	
Lime Park Rd. PE17	13 C7	
Limes Ct. PE17	13 C7	
Lincoln Av. PE17	12 C2	
Lincoln Clo. PE18	18 B4	
Linden Gro. PE18	9 C2	
Lindeth Clo. PE18	6 B3	
Lingmoor. PE18	6 B4	
Link Dri. PE18	8 A2	
Links Way. PE17	12 C4	
Linsay Clo. PE17	10 B1	
Lions Cross. PE18	9 D3	
Lions Yd. PE18	18 B5	
Literary Wk. PE18	3 C2	
Little Farthing Clo. PE17	13 E5	
Little How. PE17	12 B2	
Little Moor. PE18	18 C2	
Littlefield Clo. PE18	9 D3	
Lodge Clo. PE18	6 C6	
Lomax Dri. PE18	8 B2	
London Rd, Godmanchester. PE18	9 D3	
London Rd, St Ives. PE17	13 C7	
London St. PE18	9 C3	
Long La. PE18	11 E3	
Longstaff Way. PE18	7 G4	
Lorna Ct. PE17	12 B2	
Love La. PE17	10 B5	
Low Rd, St Ives. PE17	13 C7	
Low Rd, Little Stukeley. PE17	5 G6	
Low Rd, Fenstanton. PE18	18 B1	
Loweswater. PE18	6 C5	
Lowry Clo. PE17	12 D2	
Loxley Grn. PE17	10 A5	
Lucas Clo. PE18	7 F3	
Lucks La. PE18	18 B5	
Lysander Clo. PE17	12 C2	
Macbeth Clo. PE18	7 F3	
Madeley Ct. PE18	11 E2	
*Magdalene Hall, St Ives Business Pk. PE18	12 F4	
Main St. PE18	7 G4	
Malecoff. PE18	9 C4	
Malthouse Clo. PE18	3 C3	
Manchester Pl. PE18	3 B2	
Manchester Rd. PE18	8 C5	
Manchester Way. PE17	12 C1	
Mandeville Rd. PE18	8 B3	
Manor Clo, Brampton. PE18	8 D4	
Manor Clo, Buckden. PE18	18 B5	
Manor Clo, Houghton. PE17	10 A4	
Manor Dri. PE18	18 B1	
Manor Gdns. PE18	18 B5	
Manor La. PE17	4 C4	
Manor Mews. PE17	13 D5	
Manor Rd. PE18	11 D2	
Maple Clo. PE17	19 A3	
Maple Dri, Huntingdon. PE18	7 E2	
Maple Dri, Little Stukeley. PE17	5 H6	
Maple End. PE17	4 C5	
Margarets Way. PE18	6 C3	
Margetts. PE18	11 F3	
Market Hill, Huntingdon. PE18	3 B2	
Market Hill, St Ives. PE17	13 D5	
*Market La, Market Hill. PE17	13 D5	
Market Rd. PE17	13 D5	
Marlborough Clo. PE17	12 C2	
Marley Rd. PE17	12 B1	
Marsh La. PE18	11 E3	
Martin Clo. PE18	9 D4	
Maryland Av. PE18	7 F2	
Maule Clo. PE18	7 E4	
Mayfield. PE18	18 B5	
Mayfield Cres. PE18	7 F4	
Mayfield Rd. PE18	7 F4	
Maytrees. PE17	13 C7	
Meadow Clo, Hemingford Grey. PE18	11 E1	
Meadow Clo, St Ives. PE17	13 E5	
Meadow Drove. PE18	19 F2	
Meadow How. PE17	12 B2	
Meadow La, Earith. PE17	19 E3	
Meadow La, Hemingford Abbots. PE18	11 B1	
Meadow La, Hemingford Grey. PE18	11 E1	
Meadow La, Houghton. PE17	10 B4	

Meadow La, St Ives. PE17   13 D5
Meadow Way, Earith. PE17   19 F3
Meadow Way, Godmanchester. PE18   9 D2
Medway Rd. PE18   7 E3
Meeting Wk. PE17   19 B4
Megs Clo. PE17   19 B4
Mere Way. PE17   10 B4
Merlin Clo. PE18   7 G3
Merritt St. PE18   6 D5
Merryland. PE17   13 D5
Merton Wk. PE18   9 D3
Michigan Rd. PE17   12 B3
Middle Miss Vw. PE18   9 C4
Midgehall Ct. PE18   6 C2
Mill Clo, Hartford. PE18   7 G3
Mill Clo, Hemingford Grey. PE18   11 E2
Mill Clo, Little Stukeley. PE17   5 G6
Mill Common. PE18   3 B3
Mill La, Bluntisham. PE17   19 B3
Mill La, Hemingford Grey. PE18   11 E2
Mill Rd, Alconbury. PE17   4 C5
Mill Rd, Buckden. PE18   18 C5
Mill Rd, Fenstanton. PE18   18 D3
Mill Rd, Hartford. PE18   7 G4
Mill Rd, Little Stukeley. PE17   5 G6
Mill St. PE17   10 B5
Miller Clo. PE18   9 C4
Miller Way. PE18   8 B2
Millfield Ct. PE18   3 A2
Milton Clo, Huntingdon. PE18   7 E3
Milton Clo, St Ives. PE17   12 C2
Moats Way. PE18   11 A4
Monet Clo. PE17   12 D1
Monks Cotts. PE18   18 C5
Montagu Rd. PE18   3 D2
Montague Rd. PE18   8 B5
Moorhouse Dri. PE18   7 E3
Morland Way. PE17   12 C1
Morris Clo. PE18   18 B6
Mowlands. PE18   9 D3
Myrtle Way. PE17   12 D4

Needingworth Rd. PE17   12 E4
Nelson Rd. PE18   7 F4
Nene Rd. PE18   7 E2
Nene Way. PE17   12 D2
New Rd, Hemingford Abbots. PE18   11 B4
New Rd, St Ives. PE17   13 D6
New St. PE18   9 C2
*Newham Hall, St Ives Business Pk. PE17   12 F4
Newnham Clo. PE18   7 F3
Newton Ct. PE18   3 C2
Nicholas La. PE17   13 C5
Nightingale Clo. PE18   7 G4
Nimrod Dri. PE17   10 B1
Norfolk Rd, Huntingdon. PE18   7 E2
Norfolk Rd, St Ives. PE17   12 C1
Norfolk Rd, Wyton. PE17   10 C1
Norman Ct. PE18   11 D2
Norris Rd. PE17   13 D5
North Rd, Alconbury Weston. PE17   4 B4
North Rd, Brampton. PE18   8 C4
North Rd, St Ives. PE17   13 C5
North Side. PE18   6 D4
North St. PE18   7 E5
Nuffield Rd. PE17   12 E3
Nursery Gdns. PE17   12 E4
Nursery Rd. PE18   3 C1
Nursery Walk. PE18   8 B2

Oak Dri. PE18   8 B2
Oak End. PE17   4 C5
Oak Tree Clo. PE17   12 C3
Oak Tree Ct. PE18   9 C3
Oakfields. PE18   11 D2
Oaklands. PE18   18 C2
Oakleigh Cres. PE18   9 C3
Oberon Clo. PE18   7 G3
Old Church La. PE17   19 B1
Old Ct. PE18   9 C2
Old Farm Ct. PE17   19 A3
Old Glebe. PE17   4 C4
Old Houghton Rd. PE18   7 H4
Old Pound Clo. PE18   11 F2
Old Ramsey Rd. PE17   13 D5
Oliver Rd. PE18   8 B3
Olivia Rd. PE18   8 B3

Orchard Cres. PE17   19 E3
Orchard End. PE17   19 B4
Orchard Gdns. PE18   18 B2
Orchard La, Brampton. PE18   8 C3
Orchard La, Huntingdon. PE18   3 D3
Orchard Ter. PE17   13 D5
Orchard Way. PE18   9 C2
Orthwaite. PE18   6 B4
Orwell Clo. PE17   12 D2
Osier Holt. PE17   19 C1
Osprey Clo. PE18   7 G2
Othello Clo. PE18   7 F3
Ouse Rd. PE17   12 D2
Ouse Wk. PE18   3 D2
Overwater Ct. PE18   6 A3
Owl Way. PE18   7 G3
Oxford Rd. PE17   13 D5
Oxmoor La. PE18   7 E4

Pages Way. PE18   8 B2
Palmers La. PE18   4 C6
Paragon Rd. PE18   12 C4
Parcell Wk. PE18   9 C4
Park Av. PE17   13 D5
Park End. PE18   18 C5
Park La, Brampton. PE18   8 B5
Park La, Godmanchester. PE18   9 C2
Park Rd, Brampton. PE18   8 B4
Park Rd, Buckden. PE18   18 C5
Park Rd, St Ives. PE17   13 E5
Park View. PE17   6 A1
Parkside. PE17   13 D5
Parkway. PE17   12 D4
Parrens Rd. PE17   19 E3
Parsons Grn. PE17   12 F4
Pathfinder Way. PE18   10 B1
Peaks Clo. PE18   6 B5
Pear Tree Clo. PE18   18 A3
Peate Clo. PE18   9 D3
Pembroke Clo, Hartford. PE18   7 F3
Pembroke Clo, St Ives. PE17   13 B6
*Pembroke Hall, St Ives Business Pk. PE17   12 F4
Pennington Rd. PE18   7 F2
Pepys Rd. PE18   8 D3
Peregrine Clo. PE18   7 G2
Perry Rd. PE18   18 A5
*Peterhouse Hall, St Ives Business Pk. PE17   12 F4
Petit Rd. PE18   9 E3
Pettis Rd. PE18   12 B2
Pettis Wk. PE18   12 B2
Pig La. PE17   12 D4
Pinder Clo. PE18   9 D4
Pinfold La. PE18   9 C3
Pipers La. PE18   9 C3
Polecat La. PE17   4 B4
Poplar Clo. PE17   7 E3
Porch Clo. PE18   9 C3
Post St. PE18   9 C2
Pound Rd. PE18   11 E3
Presses Clo. PE17   19 B3
Primrose La. PE18   3 D1
Princes St. PE18   3 B2
Pringle Ct. PE17   5 G5
Pringle Way. PE17   5 G5
Priors Rd. PE18   11 D3
Priory Gro. PE18   3 C1
Priory La. PE18   7 E4
Priory Rd, Huntingdon. PE18   3 C1
Priory Rd, St Ives. PE17   13 D6
Prospero Way. PE18   7 F3
Provence Rd. PE18   6 B3

*Quay Ct, The Quay. PE17   13 D6
Queens Clo. PE18   12 B1
Queens Dri. PE18   7 F5

Ramsey Rd. PE17   12 B1
Ravenside. PE18   9 E3
Rectory Clo. PE18   8 D3
Rectory Gdns. PE18   9 D2
Rectory La. PE17   10 A5
Rectory Rd. PE17   19 B4
Red Lion Clo. PE17   4 C5
Redlands. PE18   18 C2
Redmoor Clo. PE17   12 D2
Redwell Clo. PE17   12 B3
Redwongs Way. PE18   6 D3
Rembrandt Way. PE17   12 D1
Renoir Clo. PE17   12 C2

Reynolds Clo. PE17   12 C2
Rhymers Gate. PE17   10 A5
Ribble Clo. PE17   12 D2
Richmond Clo. PE18   7 E1
Riddiford Cres. PE18   8 B3
Rideaway. PE18   11 B1
Rideaway Dri. PE18   11 B2
River La. PE18   8 D5
River Meadow. PE18   11 B1
*Rivermill House, The Quay. PE17   13 D5
Riverside Rd. PE18   3 D3
Robbs Wk. PE17   13 D5
Robin Ter. PE17   4 C5
Rodney Rd. PE18   7 F4
Roman Way. PE18   9 D4
Romney Clo. PE17   12 C2
Rookery Clo. PE17   12 E4
Rookery Pl. PE18   18 C2
Rookery Way. PE18   18 C2
Roscrea Ct. PE18   3 A2
Roscrea Ter. PE18   3 A2
Rosenthall Ter. PE18   11 E2
Rowan Clo. PE18   6 D5
Royal Oak La. PE18   11 B1
Royal Oak Pass. PE18   3 B2
Rubens Way. PE17   12 C2
Rushes Wk. PE18   9 D3
Rushington Clo. PE17   12 E3
Rusts La. PE17   4 C5
Rutland Clo. PE17   12 C1
Rydal Clo. PE18   6 C4

Saddlers Way. PE18   11 F3
*St Anns Ct, St Anns La. PE18   9 C2
St Anns La. PE18   9 C2
St Audrey Clo. PE17   12 E4
St Audrey La. PE17   12 D4
St Barnabas St. PE18   7 F3
St Benedicts Ct. PE18   3 C2
*St Catherines Hall, St Ives Business Pk. PE17   12 F4
St Clements Pass. PE18   3 C3
St Georges Ct. PE18   3 B2
St Georges Rd. PE17   13 C5
St Germain St. PE18   3 C2
St Hughs Rd. PE18   18 B4
*St Ives Rd, Hemingford Grey. PE18   11 E2
St Ives Rd, Houghton. PE17   10 B5
St James St. PE18   11 E2
*St Johns Hall, St Ives Business Pk. PE17   12 F4
St Johns Rd. PE17   13 D5
St Johns St. PE18   3 A1
St Johns Ter. PE18   6 D5
St Margarets Rd. PE17   10 A4
St Marys. PE17   19 F2
St Marys Clo. PE18   19 B4
St Marys Ct. PE18   3 C3
St Marys Rd. PE18   19 B3
St Marys St. PE18   3 C3
St Peters Rd. PE18   6 D3
Salisbury Clo. PE17   12 C1
Sallowbush Rd. PE18   7 E3
Sallows. PE18   18 C1
Salon Way. PE18   6 B3
Sandwich Clo. PE17   12 C1
Sandwich Clo. PE18   7 E3
Sandwich Rd. PE18   8 B4
Sapley Pk. PE18   7 F2
Sapley Rd. PE18   7 F1
Sapley Sq. PE18   7 E2
Saunders Clo. PE17   5 G6
Saunders Clo. PE18   7 E3
Sawtry Way. PE17   10 A1
Saxon Clo. PE18   9 C3
Sayer St. PE18   6 D5
Sayers Clo. PE18   19 B3
Scholars Av. PE18   6 C6
School La, Alconbury. PE17   4 C4
School La, Buckden. PE18   18 C1
School La, Fenstanton. PE18   18 C1
School La, Hartford. PE18   7 G4
School Rd. PE17   19 E3
Scorney. PE18   18 C1
Scrolans. PE17   12 B2
Sears Clo. PE18   9 C3
Seathwaite. PE18   6 B4
Second Drove. PE17   13 E6
Selby Clo. PE18   7 F2
*Selwyn Hall, St Ives Business Pk. PE17   12 F4

Shakespeare Rd. PE17   12 B
Sharp Clo. PE17   12 B
Sharps La. PE17   4 C
Sheepfold. PE17   12 E
Shelley Clo. PE18   7 F
Short Drove. PE17   19 F
Short La. PE17   19 A
*Sidney Sussex Hall, St Ives Business Pk. PE17   12 F
Silver Birch Av. PE17   12 C
Silver Birch Clo. PE18   7 E
Silver St, Buckden. PE18   18 B
Silver St, Godmanchester. PE18   9 C
Simmer Piece. PE18   18 C
Skeels Ct. PE18   7 F
Skeggles Clo. PE18.   6 C
Skelton Pl. PE17   12 D
Sleepe Ct. PE17   13 D
Smith Dri. PE18   18 C
Snowdonia Way. PE18   6 B
Snowy Way. PE18   7 H
Sokemans Way. PE18   8 B
Somerset Rd. PE17   10 C
Somersham Rd. PE17   12 E
South Rd. PE18   8 C
South Side. PE18   6 D
South St. PE18   7 F
Sparrow Clo, Brampton. PE18   8 B
Sparrow Clo, Huntingdon. PE18   7 E
Sparrow Dri. PE17   4 C
Sparrowhawk Way. PE18   7 G
Spencer Dri. PE17   12 C
Spinney Clo. PE18   8 C
Spinney La. PE17   4 C
Spinney Way. PE17   12 C
Spires End. PE17   4 B
Spitfire Clo. PE18   6 B
Spittals Way. PE18   6 C
Splash La. PE17   10 A
Spring Clo. PE18   7 E
Springfield. PE18   7 E
Springfield Clo. PE18   18 B
Springfield Rd. PE17   4 A
Stanpoint Way. PE18   12 D
Stanton Way. PE18   6 C
Starling Clo. PE17   4 C
Station Rd, Bluntisham. PE17   19 A
Station Rd, St Ives. PE17   13 D
Stephenson Rd. PE17   12 E
Stepping Stones. PE18   11 F
Stickle Clo. PE18   6 B
Stirling Rd. PE17   12 C
Stirtloe La. PE18   18 B
Stonehill. PE18   6 C
Stoney Clo. PE18   7 F
Stour Clo. PE17   12 D
Stuart Clo. PE18   9 D
Stubbs Clo. PE17   12 C
Stukeley Rd. PE18   6 C
Suffolk Clo, Huntingdon. PE18   7 F
Suffolk Clo, St Ives. PE17   12 C
Surrey Rd. PE18   7 E
Sussex Rd. PE17   10 B
Swan Clo. PE17   12 B
Swan End. PE18   18 C
Swan Gdns. PE18   18 C
Sweetings Rd. PE18   9 C
Sycamore Dri. PE18   7 E
Sylton Clo. PE18   9 D

Talls La. PE18   18 C
Tamar Clo. PE17   12 D
Tanglewood. PE17   4 B
Tawny Cres. PE18   7 H
Tay Clo. PE17   12 E
Taylors La. PE18   18 B
Teal Clo. PE17   12 B
Temple Clo. PE18   3 D
Tennis Court Av. PE18   3 D
Tennyson Av. PE17   12 B
Tennyson Clo. PE18   7 F
Tenterleas. PE18   13 D
Thackray Clo. PE18   7 E
Thames Rd. PE18   7 F
The Acre. PE17   4 C
The Apple Orchard. PE18   11 F
The Avenue. PE18   9 C
The Barns. PE18   18 C

ST. NEOTS

Hawkesford Way. PE19 15 F5
Hawthorn Clo. PE19 15 E2
Hawthorn Rd. PE19 15 E6
Hayling Av. PE19 15 F2
Hempsals. PE19 17 F2
Hen Brook. PE19 14 C6
Heron Ct. PE19 17 F2
High St, Hail Weston. PE19 14 A3
High St, Little Paxton. PE19 15 E2
High St, St Neots. PE19 3 B5
Hill Rise. PE19 15 G6
Hogarth Pl. PE19 14 C6
Honeydon Av. PE19 16 B1
Howard Rd. PE19 16 B5
Howitts Gdns. PE19 17 F4
Howitts La. PE19 17 F2
Humberley Clo. PE19 17 E3
Huntingdon Rd. PE19 15 F5
Huntingdon St. PE19 3 C5
*Hydropore Ho, Alington Rd
  Business Pk. PE19 17 E5

INDUSTRIAL ESTATES:
  Admiral Ct
    Business Pk. PE19 17 E5
  Alington Rd
    Business Pk. PE19 17 E5
  Howard Rd Ind Est. PE19 16 C4
Ingles Ct. PE19 3 C4
Inkerman Rise. PE19 16 C1
Ireton Clo. PE19 17 F2
Ivel Clo. PE19 16 C2

James Ct. PE19 17 F4
Jellicoe Pl. PE19 16 A3
Jenkins Clo. PE19 16 A3
*Jimea Ho, Alington Rd
  Business Pk. PE19 17 E5
Jubilee Clo. PE19 15 F2
Jutland Rise. PE19 16 C1

Keats Ct. PE19 14 C6
Kenilworth Clo. PE19 16 C3
*Keppal Ho, Alington Rd
  Business Pk. PE19 17 E5
Kestrel Pl. PE19 15 G5
Kimbolton Rd. PE19 14 A3
Kings La. PE19 3 D4
Kings Rd,
  Eaton Socon. PE19 16 B2
Kings Rd, St Neots. PE19 3 D4
Kipling Pl. PE19 14 D6
Knaresborough Ct. PE19 17 F5
Knights Clo. PE19 16 B2
Kym Rd. PE19 16 C2

Lady Way. PE19 16 B1
Lakefield Av. PE19 15 F2
Lakeside Clo. PE19 15 F2
Lammas Way. PE19 15 E6
Langwood Clo. PE19 14 C6
Lansbury Clo. PE19 17 E2
Laurel Clo. PE19 17 F2
Lawrence Rd. PE19 16 C1
Laxton Clo. PE19 16 C1
Levellers La. PE19 17 F3
Leys Rd. PE19 15 E6
Lime Gro. PE19 15 E6
Linclare Pl. PE19 16 C2
Lindisfarne Clo. PE19 17 F5
Linley Rd. PE19 17 E2
Little End Rd. PE19 16 B4
Little Paxton La. PE19 15 E2
Longfellow Pl. PE19 16 D1
Longsands Rd. PE19 15 G6
Lottings Way. PE19 14 C6
Lowry Rd. PE19 14 C6
Luke St. PE19 17 E2
*Maddison Ho,
  Bedford St. PE19 3 B4

*Malden Ho,
  Bedford St. PE19 3 B4
Mallard La. PE19 3 D6
Manor Clo. PE19 15 E2
Manor Farm Rd. PE19 17 G1
Manor Gro. PE19 17 F1
Manor Ho Clo. PE19 16 B3
Manor Pk. PE19 17 F1
Manor Way. PE19 14 A3
Marchioness Way. PE19 16 B2
Market Sq. PE19 3 A5
Marlowe Ct. PE19 14 D5
Marquis Clo. PE19 16 B2
Marshall Rd. PE19 3 D6
Marston Rd. PE19 17 F2
Masefield Av. PE19 14 C6
Meadow Clo,
  Little Paxton. PE19 15 E2
Meadow Clo, St Neots. PE19 3 C6
Meadowsweet. PE19 14 B6
Medallion Ct. PE19 3 C5
Medland Gro. PE19 3 D6
Merlin Clo. PE19 15 H5
Mill Hill Rd. PE19 16 C1
Mill La. PE19 15 E3
Milton Av. PE19 14 C5
Minden Clo. PE19 16 C1
Monarch Rd. PE19 16 A2
Montagu St. PE19 17 E2
Moores Wk. PE19 3 B5
Mountbatten Ct. PE19 16 C2
Mountfort Clo. PE19 17 E3
Mullien Clo. PE19 14 C6
Muntjac Clo. PE19 16 B1
Murrell Clo. PE19 15 F5
Murrell Ct. PE19 15 F5
Musgrave Way. PE19 3 D6

Naseby Gdns. PE19 17 F2
Navigation Wharf. PE19 3 B6
*Nelson Ho, Alington Rd
  Business Pk. PE19 17 E5
Nelson Rd. PE19 16 B3
Nene Rd. PE19 16 C2
New St. PE19 3 B4
Newtown Rd. PE19 14 B3
Nightingale Way. PE19 15 H5
Northfield Rd. MK44 16 A5
Nursery Rd. PE19 3 D6

Oak Clo. PE19 15 G6
Ockenden Clo. PE19 16 B3
Old School Gdns. PE19 16 C4
Orchard Clo,
  Eaton Ford. PE19 16 C1
Orchard Clo,
  Hail Weston. PE19 14 A3
Orchard Rd. PE19 16 C1
Orchid Clo. PE19 14 C6
Osier Ct. PE19 14 C5
Otter Way. PE19 16 B1
Ouse Rd. PE19 16 C2

Paines Mill. PE19 3 B4
Park Av. PE19 15 E2
Park Clo. PE19 15 E2
Park Cres. PE19 15 E2
Park Dri. PE19 15 E3
Park Rd. PE19 15 F5
Park View Ct. PE19 16 D1
Parkside. PE19 15 E2
Parkway, Little Paxton. PE19 15 E2
Parkway, St Neots. PE19 15 F5
Paxton Ct. PE19 15 F2
Peer Rd. PE19 16 B1
Pembroke Av. PE19 17 E4
Penrwyn Ct. PE19 17 E4
*Peppercorn Ho,
  New St. PE19 3 B5

Peppercorn La. PE19 16 B3
Pepys Rd. PE19 17 F1
Philip Gdns. PE19 17 F4
Phoenix Sq. PE19 3 B4
Pope Rd. PE19 17 E2
Popham Clo. PE19 16 A3
Potton Rd. PE19 17 F3
Pound Clo. PE19 14 B3
Powis Pl. PE19 17 E4
Prince Clo. PE19 16 B1
Princes Dri. PE19 3 D4
Priory Hill Rd. PE19 15 G4
Priory La. PE19 3 A5
Priory Mall. PE19 3 A5
Priory Rd. PE19 3 A4
Prospect Row. PE19 3 C5

Queens Ct. PE19 16 B2
Queens Gdns. PE19 16 B2
Queensway. PE19 15 E5

Rampley Clo. PE19 15 E3
Rampley La. PE19 15 E1
Raven Clo. PE19 15 G5
Redwing Pl. PE19 15 H5
Regent Clo. PE19 16 B2
Reynolds Ct. PE19 14 C6
Reynolds Dri. PE19 15 F3
Richmond Clo. PE19 17 E5
Ridgeway. PE19 17 E3
River Clo. PE19 15 E3
River Rd. PE19 16 C2
River Ter. PE19 3 A6
Rivers Mead. PE19 15 E5
Roe Grn. PE19 16 B1
Romney Ct. PE19 14 C6
Rookery Rd. MK44 16 A5
Rose Ct. PE19 16 C2
Rowley Rd. PE19 15 G5
Royal Ct. PE19 16 B2
Russell Ct. PE19 3 C4
Russell St. PE19 3 B4
Rycroft Av. PE19 3 B4
Rye Clo. PE19 17 F4

St Anselm Pl. PE19 3 A4
St James Rd. PE19 15 F1
St Marys Ct. PE19 3 B6
St Marys St. PE19 3 B6
St Neots Rd. PE19 3 A6
Sambar Clo. PE19 16 B1
Sandfields Rd. PE19 3 D6
Sandwich Rd. PE19 15 G6
Saviles Clo. PE19 14 D5
Saxon Pl. PE19 17 E1
School La,
  Eaton Socon. PE19 16 B4
School La,
  Little Paxton. PE19 15 F2
School La, St Neots. PE19 17 E1
Setchel. PE19 14 C6
Shaftesbury Av. PE19 3 D5
Shakespeare Rd. PE19 16 B3
Shelley Pl. PE19 14 D6
Shirdley Rd. PE19 17 E2
Silvan Clo. PE19 15 E3
Silver St. PE19 17 E2
Silverweed. PE19 14 C6
Simpkin Clo. PE19 16 B4
South St. PE19 3 B5
Spencer Clo. PE19 14 D6
Spring Pl. PE19 14 A3
Springbrook. PE19 17 F2
Springfield Clo. PE19 15 F6
Squires Clo. PE19 16 B2
Station Rd. PE19 15 G6
Staughton Pl. PE19 16 C1
Steel Clo. PE19 16 B4
Stevenson Ct. PE19 14 D6
Stratford Pl. PE19 16 C3

Sundew Clo. PE19 14 B
Sunnybank. PE19 15 F
Swallow Ct. PE19 15 G
Sweeting Av. PE19 15 F
Swift Clo. PE19 15 G

Tan Yd. PE19 3 B
Tansur Ct. PE19 15 F
Tansy Clo. PE19 14 B
Tavistock Ct. PE19 3 B
Teasel Clo. PE19 14 B
Tebbutts Rd. PE19 3 B
Tenby Way. PE19 17 F
Tennyson Pl. PE19 14 D
Tern Way. PE19 15 G
Teversham Way. PE19 14 C
The Broad Walk. PE19 17 E
The Close. PE19 3 C
The Crescent,
  Eaton Socon. PE19 16 C
The Crescent,
  St Neots. PE19 15 E
The Crofts. PE19 15 F
The Grove. PE19 15 E
The Hallards. PE19 14 C
The Hives. PE19 16 C
The Maltings. PE19 16 C
The Orchard. PE19 15 E
The Paddock. PE19 16 D
The Priory. PE19 3 A
The Rookery. PE19 15 F
The Sycamores,
  Little Paxton. PE19 15 E
The Sycamores,
  St Neots. PE19 3 C
Tintagel Ct. PE19 17 E
Topham Ct. PE19 15 F
Trafalgar Rd. PE19 16 C
Turner Rd. PE19 14 C

Valarian Clo. PE19 14 C
*Vernon Ho, Alington Rd
  Business Pk. PE19 17 E
Viceroy Clo. PE19 16 A
*Vincent Ho, Alington Rd
  Business Pk. PE19 17 E
Viscount Ct. PE19 16 B
Vulcan Way. PE19 16 B

Wantage Gdns. PE19 15 F
Ware Rd. PE19 3 B
Warwick Ct. PE19 16 C
Washbank Rd. PE19 17 E
Waterloo Dri. PE19 17 E
Waterside Ct. PE19 3 B
Welland Ct. PE19 16 C
West St. PE19 3 B
Weston Clo. PE19 14 A
Weston Ct. PE19 16 C
Wheatsheaf Rd. PE19 14 C
Whistler Rd. PE19 14 C
Whitehall Wk. PE19 17 F
Wildber Clo. PE19 17 E
Wilkinson Clo. PE19 16 B
William Rd. PE19 17 F
Willow Clo, Eynesbury. PE19 17 F
Willow Clo,
  Little Paxton. PE19 15 F
Windmill Row. PE19 3 B
Windsor Clo. PE19 17 F
Wintringham Rd. PE19 3 D
Wistow Ct. PE19 14 C
Woodlands. PE19 15 G
Wordsworth Av. PE19 14 D
Wyboston Ct. PE19 16 B